*For the Wesley Ringers of McFarlin Memorial United Methodist Church,*

# Basic Training for Bells
## Skill Building for Ringers

### By Venita MacGorman
#### With Erin MacGorman

**2-3 octaves Handbells or Handchimes**

**Music and Literary Editors**
*Kathy Lowrie and Jeff Reeves*

**Graphic Design**
*Leon Graphics*

**Cover Design and Illustrations**
*Travis Foster*

**Photography**
*William Weinkauf*

*Copyright © 2003 Choristers Guild. All rights reserved. Printed in U.S.A. Reproduction of all or any portion in any form is prohibited without permission of the publisher.*

*www.choristersguild.org*

*Published by Choristers Guild, 2834 W. Kingsley Road, Garland, Texas 75041-2498*
*Distributed by the Lorenz Corporation, 501 E. Third Street, Box 802, Dayton, Ohio 45401-0801*

**The CCLI license does not grant permission to photocopy this music.**

# Introduction

We use many skills when we ring in a handbell choir. Ringing the bell, reading the music, counting the rhythms and playing as an ensemble are all essential skills for the beginning group. Educators tell us that new skills are best learned by breaking them up into their component parts and then teaching those parts consecutively. Ringers tell us that they just want to ring bells and make music!

This book is an attempt to teach the essential skills needed for beginning ringers by presenting rote exercises to drill each new skill followed by a musical piece that uses that skill. By using rote drills, we eliminate the need for reading music at the same time we learn new ringing techniques. Each musical selection contains only those skills which have been previously presented. Rote drills involve the entire bell choir and the musical selections present each new technique or rhythm in both treble and bass clefs so that ALL of the ringers learn ALL of the skills. Although the exercises were originally developed for three octave handbell choirs, instructions are given to adapt the exercises to handchime choirs or for use with two octave groups. Each musical selection appears in both two octave and three octave versions.

It is our hope that beginning handbell choirs will find in this collection music that can be used in the very early weeks of rehearsals and that will build the needed skills before they are encountered in the music. Be sure to review the rote exercises and related music found in each skill as needed. This will help to reinforce lessons already learned and bolster the confidence of new ringers.

The exercises have been developed over a period of several years, as they were needed for beginning groups. The musical selections have been "field tested" with a beginning group of sixth graders, whose patience we greatly appreciate!

Venita and Erin MacGorman

# Contents

Skill 1: Ringing the Bell — **4**

Skill 2: Ringing as an Ensemble — **5**

Skill 3: Damping as an Ensemble — **12**

Skill 4: Changing Bells — **17**

Skill 5: Playing at Different Dynamic Levels — **28**

Skill 6: The Shake — **31**

Skill 7: Reading and Ringing Eighth Notes and Eighth Rests — **34**

Skill 8: Stopped Techniques — **37**

Skill 9: Playing in 3/4 and 2/4 Meters — **43**

Skill 10: Reading and Ringing Dotted Rhythms — **48**

Skill 11: The Echo — **56**

Skill 12: The Swing — **59**

Skill 13: Let Vibrate — **68**

Skill 14: Martellato and Martellato Lift — **71**

Skill 15: Using Mallets — **79**

List of Choristers Guild Handbell Music — **92**
(Levels 1 and 2) with related techniques

Index of Songs — **96**

# Skill One
## Ringing the Bell

### Before the Ringers Arrive

Prepare the rehearsal room before each rehearsal begins. Prior to the first several rehearsals, lay the bells on the table in diatonic order (all natural bells for three octave choirs; include F#5 and F#6 for two octave choirs). Consider meeting the ringers outside of the bell room door at the first rehearsal. Pass out gloves and briefly discuss how to care for and protect the bells BEFORE the ringers actually approach the bells.

### Rote Exercise #1

Assign each ringer two diatonic, natural bells. (Two octave choirs should have the F ringers take F#.) Have the ringers place their hands flat on the bells, palms down, fingers together. The thumbs move away from the fingers, making a "V" between thumb and forefinger. Now close the thumbs and fingers around the handle as if "shaking hands" with it. Keep the thumbs curved and not locked. Lift the bells to approximately shoulder height and tilt them back just enough that the clapper falls back toward the ringer. This is the "ready to ring" position.

### Rote Exercise #2

From this position, move the forearm forward and back, allowing the clapper to move forward and strike the bell. Tell the ringers to imagine there is water in the bell but avoid "spilling" it out as they ring. Allow the ringers to random ring. Move among the ringers and check for correct thumb position and arm motion.

### Rote Exercise #3

Demonstrate ringing a bell in circles of different sizes. Allow the ringers to practice this as a group. Now establish a comfortable steady beat. Have the ringers imitate you ringing notes of one, two, and four beats. Name these notes "quarter," "half," and "whole" notes. Display these notes on flash cards (as shown below) identifying them by name and beat duration.

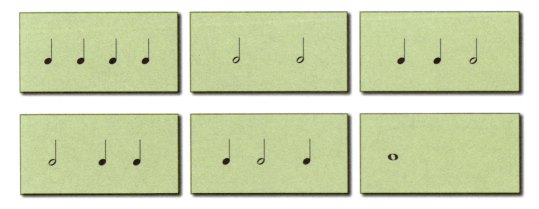

# Skill Two
## Ringing as an Ensemble

### Rote Exercise #1

Ringers take their two natural bells. (Two octave choirs should have the F ringers take F#.) Establish a comfortable steady beat. Beginning with the lowest two positions, Ringers 1 and 2 ring their left bells together twice in quarter notes, then their right bells together twice in quarter notes. Have them work to ring "as one" with the bells sounding together at exactly the same time. Also encourage the ringers to match the length of arm strokes as much as possible. Ringer 2 then repeats the pattern with ringer 3, and so on up the table. Everyone plays with both his left and right neighbor with the exception of the lowest and highest ringers, who only have one neighbor. This "Ringing in Thirds"* exercise will be used to present a variety of techniques.

### Rote Exercise #2

Ringers take their two natural bells. (Two octave choirs should have the F ringers take F#.) Ringer 1 rings a whole note with her left bell, then with her right bell, making an arm circle that takes the entire four beats. While ringer 1 does this, the remaining ringers pantomime; that is, they make the same circles with their arms and bells, but do not actually ring. After ringer 1 has rung her two bells, she begins to pantomime as ringer 2 repeats what ringer 1 has just done. Continue up the table until everyone has a turn to actually ring their bells. This exercise takes a great deal of control and may be uncomfortable at first. The goals are twofold: to draw the ringers' attention to the actual motion of ringing in a circle, and to build muscular control, which will later help in performing dynamic contrast.

---

* From *The Director as Teacher: Working with the Beginning Handbell Choir* by Venita MacGorman. Copyright © 1996 The American Guild of English Handbell Ringers, Inc. Used by permission. All rights reserved.

# Skill Two — Ringing as an Ensemble

## Reading Music on the Staff

Ringers with little or no music experience need to become comfortable with basic rhythms and note names on the staff. The following exercise will help ringers to develop those skills.

Have ringers study the music staff noting the lines and spaces. Tell them to assume that their left hand will ring the notes in a space and their right hand will ring the notes on a line. (Note names are not important at this time.) Practice "ghost ringing" (ringing without bells) the music examples below. Count aloud and/or clap the steady beat as ringers play. Encourage the ringers to "tap their toe" or count aloud as they ring. This will help them internalize the steady beat. Now have ringers take their two natural bells and practice ringing the music examples again.

Have ringers locate their two bells on the chart below. Ask them to identify the clef, line and space on which their bells (notes) appear on the staff. Ringers may wish to lightly circle and/or put their initials by their bells (notes) and refer back to this chart as needed. When ringers can easily locate their notes, proceed to the first song, "Morning Bells I." As they become comfortable ringing this piece, they will grow eager to expand their skills with the pieces that follow.

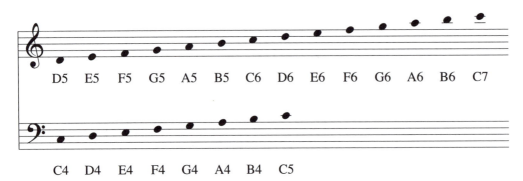

## Skill Two — Ringing as an Ensemble

### Musical Examples — Three Octaves

*"Morning Bells I" - Chords (3 oct)*

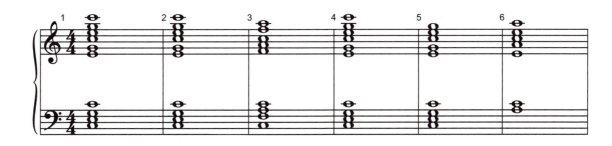

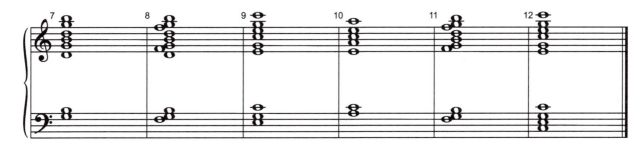

## Skill Two — Ringing as an Ensemble

*"Morning Bells II" – Treble Melody (3 oct)*

# Morning Bells II – Treble Melody
### 3 octaves

based on *WACHET AUF*
Philipp Nicolai, 1556-1608
arr. Erin MacGorman

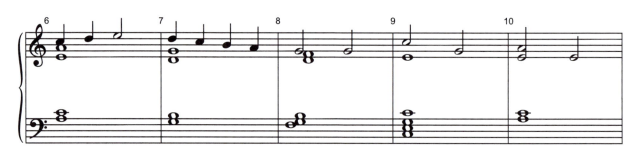
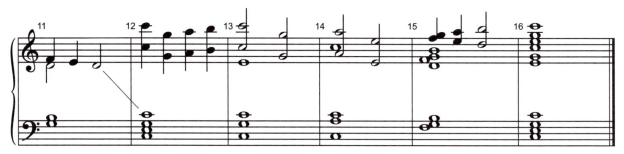

## Skill Two — Ringing as an Ensemble

*"Morning Bells III" – Bass Melody (3 oct)*

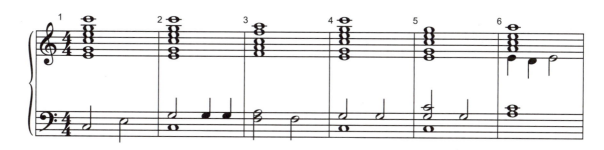

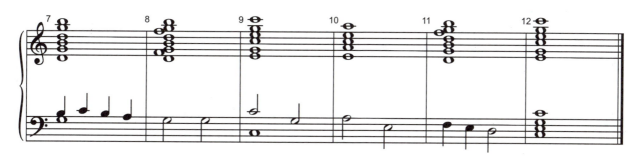

## Skill Two — Ringing as an Ensemble

### Musical Examples — Two Octaves

*"Morning Bells I" – Chords (2 oct)*

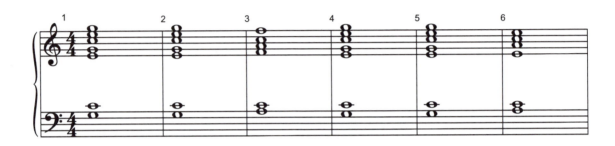

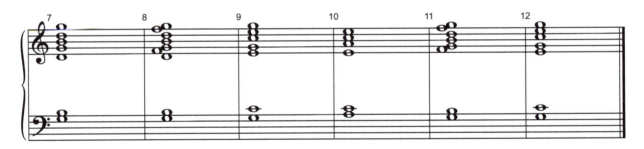

# Skill Two — Ringing as an Ensemble

*"Morning Bells II" (2 oct)*

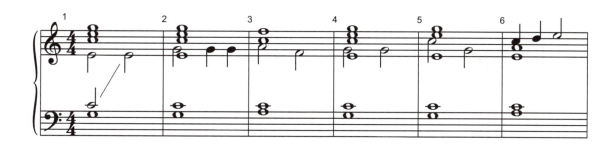

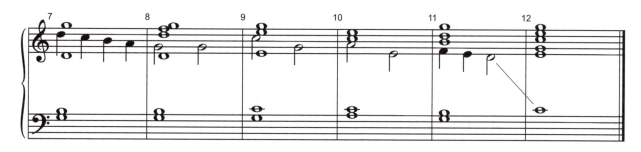

# Skill Three
## Damping as an Ensemble

### Rote Exercise #1

Ringers take their two natural bells. On cue, have all ringers play both bells together and hold for four beats. On beat five, damp all bells except C, E, and G which remain sounding for an additional four beats. Repeat this drill several times. The difference in sound between the tone cluster and the sound of the C major chord will make it immediately obvious when all bells are damped together. Repeat the exercise with other major chords: FAC, GBD.

### Rote Exercise #2

Display on flash cards the rhythm patterns below. Establish a comfortable steady beat and demonstrate ringing each pattern. Have the ringers echo you. Work to achieve immediate silence on the rests. If any bell is not fully damped, it will "hang over" and be audible. Drill the patterns until the ringers can play them successfully.

## Skill Three — Damping as an Ensemble

### Musical Examples — Three Octaves

*"Count the Rests!" (3 oct)*

## Skill Three — Damping as an Ensemble

*"God Is So Good" (3 oct)*
*(Note: This piece is not in the key of C. Ringers who play B4, B5, or B6, should play Bb4, Bb5, and Bb6 instead. Key signatures will be addressed in Skill #4.)*

## Skill Three — Damping as an Ensemble

### Musical Examples — Two Octaves

*"Count the Rests!" (2 oct)*
(Note: This piece is not in the key of C. Ringers who play F5 or F6 should play F#5 and F#6 instead. Key signatures will be addressed in Skill #4.)

Count the Rests!
2 octaves

Venita MacGorman

# Skill Three — Damping as an Ensemble

*"God Is So Good" (2 oct)*

# Skill Four
## Changing Bells

In Skill 3, both 2 and 3 octave bell choirs had the chance to play a piece in a key other than C major. Several ringers, then, had to change one of their natural bells for a sharp or flat bell. In this lesson, all ringers discover the art of changing bells and how to execute the technique properly.

Display the following bells in this order: A5, A#5, B5. Show the ringers that A#5 has one name (A#5) on one side of the bell handle and another name (Bb5) on the other side. Although the bell has two names, it only has one sound. Play the A5 bell, then the A#5 bell. Ringers should recognize that A#5 produces a higher pitch. Now play B5, then Bb5. Ringers should recognize that Bb5 produces a lower pitch. Explain that the sharp and flat bells go half way in between the naturals. Point out the bells that do not have a sharp or flat between them (E and F, B and C).

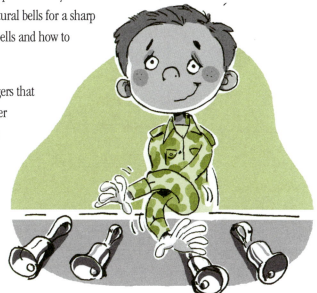

### Rote Exercise #1

Ringers take their two natural bells. Alternating left and right, ring half notes. Damp the left bell on the shoulder and the right bell on the table. (Be sure to put the lip of the bell into the foam so that the bell does not sound.) Repeat the exercise damping the left bell on the table and the right bell on the shoulder. Repeat the exercise again using quarter notes.

### Rote Exercise #2

Each ringer adds a third bell (sharp or flat) that corresponds to his natural bells. Place the third bell between the other two bells. (The bells may not be in pitch sequence.)

Ring half notes, beginning with the left bell, which is damped on the shoulder. Then ring the right bell, damp it on the table and let go of it. Move the right hand to the center bell while the left hand rings the left bell again. After the right hand rings the center bell, damp the center bell on the table, drop it, and pick up the right bell as the left bell rings. The pattern established is: Left, Right, Left, Center, Left, Right, Left, Center. Reverse the exercise so that the left hand moves between the left and center bells. Once the ringers are successful, repeat the exercise using quarter notes.

Explain that each piece of music has a key signature indicating which sharp or flat bells to play in the music. This is a good time to begin introducing key signatures and accidentals.

# Skill Four — Changing Bells

## Musical Examples — Three Octaves

*"Jesus Shall Reign – Preparatory Exercise" (3 oct)*

# Skill Four — Changing Bells

*"Jesus Shall Reign I" (3 oct)*

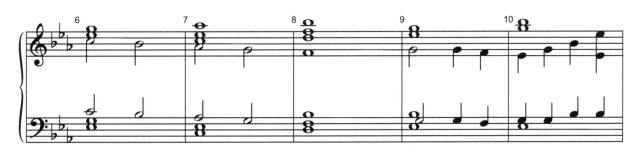

## Skill Four — Changing Bells

*"Jesus Shall Reign II" (3 oct)*

# Jesus Shall Reign II
### 3 octaves

*DUKE STREET*
attr. John Hatton, ca. 1710-1793
arr. Venita MacGorman

# Skill Four — Changing Bells

## Musical Examples — Two Octaves

*"Jesus Shall Reign – Preparatory Exercise" (2 oct)*

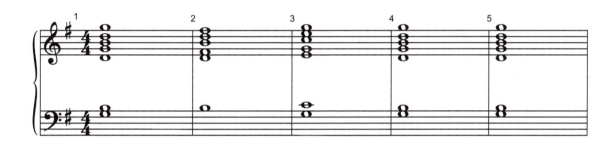

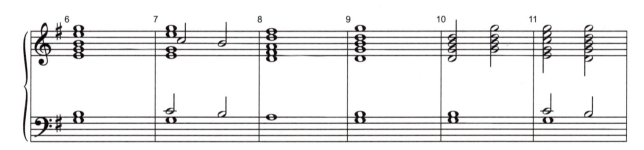

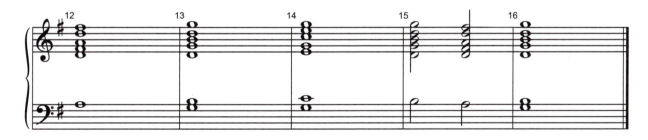

# Skill Four — Changing Bells

*"Jesus Shall Reign I" (2 oct)*

## Skill Four — Changing Bells

*"Jesus Shall Reign II" (2 oct)*

## Skill Four — Changing Bells

### Musical Example — Three Octaves
*"Happy or Sad?" (3 oct)*

# Skill Four — Changing Bells

*"Happy or Sad?" (3 oct)* continued

25

# Skill Four — Changing Bells

## Musical Example — Two Octaves
*"Happy or Sad?" (2 oct)*

# Skill Four — Changing Bells

*"Happy or Sad?" (2 oct)* continued

27

# Skill Five
## Playing at Different Dynamic Levels*

### Rote Exercise #1

Ringers take their right, natural bell. In quarter notes, ring this bell ten times, gradually increasing the dynamic level with each strike of the bell (1=soft as possible; 10=loud as possible). Tell the ringers to think of using only the fingers to ring softly. To get louder, "add muscles" near the shoulder, so that the loudest ring uses every muscle in the hand and shoulder. Ringers will become aware of the "feel" of each dynamic level.

### Rote Exercise #2

Now have the ringers practice getting gradually softer by ringing from "ten to one." Start ringing as loud as possible and "take out muscles" to get progressively softer. This will be much more difficult!

### Rote Exercise #3

Repeat Exercises #1 and #2 using the left, natural bell only. Finally, have the ringers take both natural bells and practice the exercise alternating between each bell.

### Challenge Exercise

Repeat Exercises #1-3 but increase the number of repetitions from ten to fifteen, then to twenty.

---

\* From *The Director as Teacher: Working with the Beginning Handbell Choir* by Venita MacGorman. Copyright © 1996 The American Guild of English Handbell Ringers, Inc. Used by permission. All rights reserved.

# Skill Five — Playing at Different Dynamic Levels

## Musical Example — Three Octaves

*"Fairest Lord Jesus" (3 oct)*

Fairest Lord Jesus
3 octaves

ST. ELIZABETH
*Schlesische Volkslieder*, 1842
arr. Venita MacGorman

# Skill Five — Playing at Different Dynamic Levels

## Musical Example — Two Octaves

*"Fairest Lord Jesus" (2 oct)*

# Skill Six
## The Shake

**SK** The shake technique is generally used with bells G4 and higher. The larger size and heavier weight of bass bells create a challenge for bass ringers to execute this technique. Ringers with bells F4 and lower should take care not to place excessive strain on the wrist and arm when using the shake.

### Rote Exercise #1

Ringers take their right, natural bell. Have them execute a shake by rapidly moving the forearm forward and backward with a relaxed wrist so that the clapper hits both sides of the bell. Repeat the exercise using the left, natural bell. (Note: Common mistakes often made when executing the shake include ignoring the steady beat and failing to observe dynamic markings.)

### Rote Exercise #2

Review Skill 5, Rote Exercises #1 and #2 (page 28). Using the "soft to loud" exercise, have ringers replace the loudest ring with a four beat shake. With the "loud to soft" exercise, have the ringers replace the softest ring with a soft, four beat shake.

### Rote Exercise #3

Ringers take their two natural bells. Ringers 1 and 2 shake their left bells together for four beats, starting the shake near the table and gradually raising it up near shoulder level. The two ringers then repeat the exercise with their right bells. The drill continues with ringers 2 and 3, and so on up the table.

# Skill Six — The Shake

## Musical Example — Three Octaves

*"God of the Ages" (3 oct)*

# Skill Six — The Shake

## Musical Example — Two Octaves

*"God of the Ages" (2 oct)*

# Skill Seven
## Reading and Ringing Eighth Notes and Eighth Rests

### Rote Exercise #1

Divide the bell choir into two groups. Instruct group one to play quarter notes, alternating left and right bells. Have group two play two notes (2 eighth notes) for each quarter note that group one plays with the pattern Left, Left, Right, Right. Ringers should use a shorter arm stroke for the eighth notes, about half the length of the stroke used for quarter notes. Drill this pattern until ringers are successful. Then have the groups swap patterns. Name the notes the ringers have been playing as "eighth notes." Explain that the duration of an eighth note is one-half of a quarter note. That is, it takes two eighth notes to equal a quarter note.

### Rote Exercise #2

Display on flash cards the rhythm patterns below. Establish a comfortable steady beat and demonstrate the patterns by first clapping, then playing each example. Have the ringers echo you. Drill the patterns until the ringers can play them successfully.

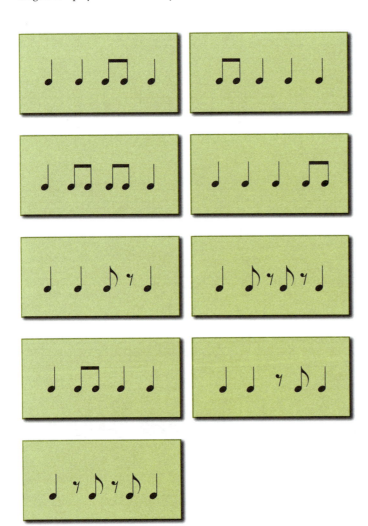

# Skill Seven — Reading and Ringing Eighth Notes and Eighth Rests

## Musical Example — Three Octaves

*"Processional" (3 oct)*

# Skill Seven — Reading and Ringing Eighth Notes and Eighth Rests

## Musical Example — Two Octaves

*"Processional" (2 oct)*

36

# Skill Eight
## Stopped Techniques

### TD Thumb Damp and PL Pluck

These two techniques are often used interchangeably. Generally, the thumb damp is more often used with treble bells while the pluck tends to be used with bass bells.

### Rote Exercise #1

To execute the thumb damp, place the thumb firmly against the side of the bell (called "casing") and ring it normally. This should result in a "stopped" sound. The sound will vary according to the amount of thumb placed on the bell. Usually, the higher bells require less thumb pressure while larger bells may require the addition of the index finger in order to stop the sound. The result should be a very short sound, but the pitch should still be clear.

### Rote Exercise #2

To execute the pluck, place the bells on the table. Grasp the clapper between the thumb and first two fingers. Throw the clapper down against the casing turning the wrist and first two fingers outwards so the hand does not interfere with the clapper movement. This is a quick, fluid motion.

### Rote Exercise # 3

Have ringers practice the thumb damp and pluck techniques using the "Ringing in Thirds" exercise (Skill 2, Rote Exercise #1, page 5).

# Skill Eight — Stopped Techniques

## Ring Touch RT

### Rote Exercise #4

Ringers take their two natural bells. (Two octave choirs may have the F ringers take F#.) Establish a steady beat and have the ringers play quarter notes, alternating left and right bells, damping one as the other rings. After repeating this several times, add a new element, the ring touch. Instruct the ringers to continue playing on the steady beat but to damp each bell as soon as it is rung. This should stop the sound and create a silence between each beat.

Challenge the ringers by changing the tempo of the steady beat (speed up/slow down). Regardless of tempo, ringers should perform the technique exactly together. This exercise teaches ringers to execute the ring touch exactly together (or the effect is lost) and to watch the director at all times.

### Note for Handchime Choirs

All stopped techniques are executed on handchimes by placing the index finger (or thumb and index finger) firmly against the tines at the "U" opening.

# Skill Eight — Stopped Techniques

## Musical Examples — Three Octaves

*"Old Ship of Zion" (3 oct)*

39

# Skill Eight — Stopped Techniques

"Dance of the Hours" (3 oct)

# Skill Eight — Stopped Techniques

## Musical Examples — Two Octaves

*"Old Ship of Zion" (2 oct)*

# Skill Eight — Stopped Techniques

*"Dance of the Hours" (2 oct)*

# Skill Nine
## Playing in Three/Four and Two/Four Meters

### Rote Exercise #1

Establish a comfortable steady beat. Demonstrate ringing a pattern of four quarter notes, accenting the first beat. Have the ringers echo you. Repeat the drill with a three beat pattern and a two beat pattern. Remember to accent beat one each time.

Explain that music can be grouped into different beat patterns where beat one is the strongest beat.

### Rote Exercise #2

Display on flash cards the rhythm patterns below. Establish a comfortable steady beat and demonstrate the patterns by first clapping, then playing each example. Have the ringers echo you. Drill the patterns until the ringers can play them successfully.

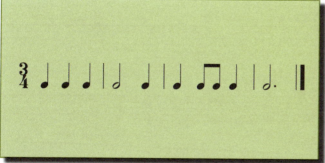

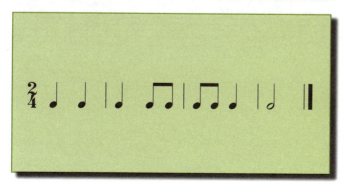

# Skill Nine — Playing in Three/Four and Two/Four Meters

## Musical Examples — Three Octaves

*"Scarborough Fair" (3 oct)*

## Skill Nine — Playing in Three/Four and Two/Four Meters

*"Little David" (3 oct)*

45

# Skill Nine — Playing in Three/Four and Two/Four Meters

## Musical Examples — Two Octaves

*"Scarborough Fair" (2 oct)*

# Skill Nine — Playing in Three/Four and Two/Four Meters

*"Little David" (2 oct)*

# Skill Ten
## Reading and Ringing Dotted Rhythms

### Rote Exercise #1

*Dotted rhythms "on the beat" (dotted half/quarter)* — Ringers take their two natural bells. Assign treble ringers to play quarter notes, alternating left and right bells. Assign bass ringers to play a dotted half note (three beats) with their left bell, then a dotted half note with their right bell. Have the two groups exchange patterns.

### Rote Exercise #2

*Dotted rhythms "off the beat" (dotted quarter/eighth)* — Assign treble ringers to play eighth notes, four with the left bell and four with the right bell. Assign bass ringers to play their left bell and listen while three eighth notes "go by." On the fourth eighth note, bass ringers ring the eighth note with the treble ringers. This gives the bass ringers the "feel" for ringing "off the beat."

Repeat the drill again, but this time, keep the drill moving (don't stop after the fourth eighth note is rung). As soon as the bass ringers ring the fourth eighth note, they should ring and immediately listen as three more eighth notes "go by." As before, bass ringers ring on the fourth eighth note with the treble ringers.

When bass ringers become comfortable ringing "off the beat," have the two groups exchange patterns. Repeat the drill giving treble ringers the chance to ring "off the beat."

### Rote Exercise #3

Display on flash cards the rhythm patterns below. Establish a comfortable steady beat and demonstrate the patterns by first clapping, then playing each example. Have the ringers echo you. Drill the patterns until the ringers can play them successfully.

# Skill Ten — Reading and Ringing Dotted Rhythms

## Musical Examples — Three Octaves

*"Lord, Have Mercy" (3 oct)*

49

### Skill Ten — Reading and Ringing Dotted Rhythms

*"Lord, Have Mercy" (3 oct)* continued

*"We, Thy People, Praise Thee" (3 oct)*

## We, Thy People, Praise Thee
3 octaves

*ST. ANTHONY CHORALE*
Franz Joseph Haydn, 1732-1809
arr. Erin MacGorman

3 octaves
Handbells used: 23

50

## Skill Ten — Reading and Ringing Dotted Rhythms

*"We, Thy People, Praise Thee"* (*3 oct*) continued

# Skill Ten — Reading and Ringing Dotted Rhythms

## Musical Examples — Two Octaves

*"Lord, Have Mercy" (2 oct)*

# Skill Ten — Reading and Ringing Dotted Rhythms

"Lord, Have Mercy" (2 oct) *continued*

# Skill Ten — Reading and Ringing Dotted Rhythms

"We, Thy People, Praise Thee (2 oct)

# Skill Ten — Reading and Ringing Dotted Rhythms

*"We, Thy People, Praise Thee (2 oct)* continued

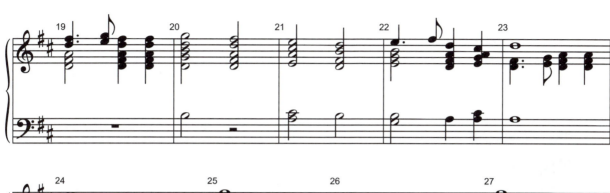

# Skill Eleven
## The Echo

**Rote Exercise**

Ringers take their two natural bells. (Two octave choirs should have the F ringers take F#.) Establish a slow steady beat. Ringer 1 plays his left bell on beat one, then touches the lip of the bell on the foam on beats two, three, and four, creating an "echo" effect. Ringer 1 repeats the drill with his right bell.

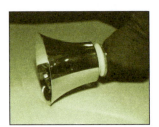

As soon as ringer 1 finishes, ringer 2 performs the exercise. However, when ringer 3 begins his turn, ringer 1 also starts the drill again. The result is a two-part round at the interval of a fifth. (This can also be done at the interval of a third.) Continue the exercise up the table experiencing the "echo" in a round.

### Note for Handchime Choirs

The echo technique can be simulated by lightly touching the forefinger to the tine of the chime and the "U" opening and then releasing it. (See photographs, page 38.)

# Skill Eleven — The Echo

## Musical Example — Three Octaves

*"Evening Prayer" (3 oct)*

# Evening Prayer
### 3 octaves

Traditional
Irish cradle song
arr. Erin MacGorman

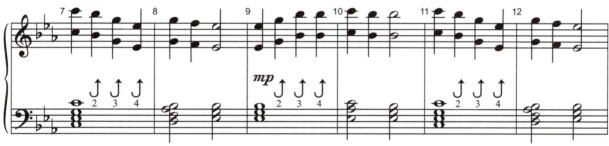

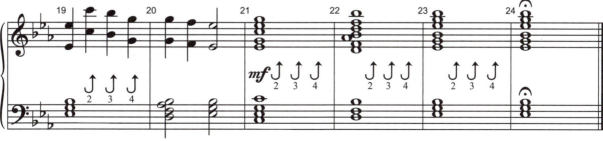

# Skill Eleven — The Echo

## Musical Example — Two Octaves

*"Evening Prayer" (2 oct)*

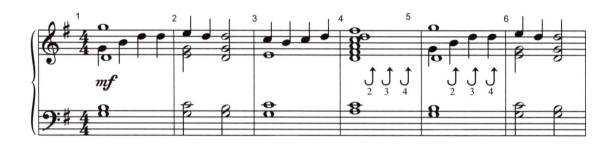

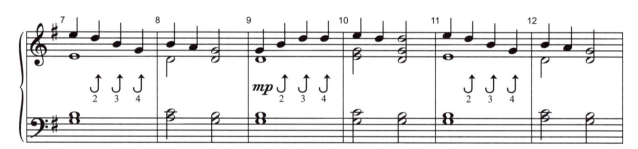

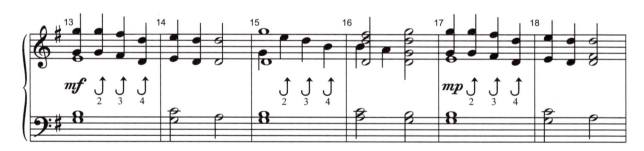

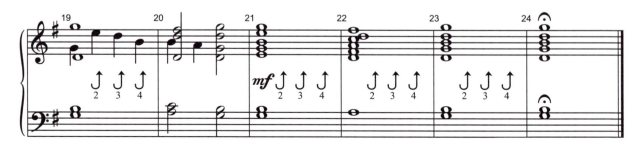

# Skill Twelve
## The Swing

### Rote Exericse #1

Ringers take their two natural bells. Have them form a circle away from the bell table (at least two arm lengths away from a wall) and rehearse the swing. Ringers will enjoy the sight and sound of the swing when they are in a circle and can see each other.

To execute the swing in a four beat pattern, ring the bell on beat one, swinging back with an extended arm on beat two, swinging forward with an extended arm on beat three, then circling up toward the shoulder on beat four. (Note: A common mistake often made when executing the swing in a four beat pattern is to damp the bell at the beginning of beat four rather than holding the note its full value.)

### Rote Exercise #2

Now rehearse the swing in a three beat pattern by ringing the bell on beat one, swinging back with an extended arm on beat two, and swinging forward AND circling up toward the shoulder on beat three.

### Rote Exercise #3

Have the ringers return to the bell table and practice alternating between three and four beat swing patterns considering the space constraints produced by the tables.

# Skill Twelve — The Swing

## Musical Examples — Three Octaves

*"On the Water I" (3 oct)*

# Skill Twelve — The Swing

*"On the Water I" (3 oct)* continued

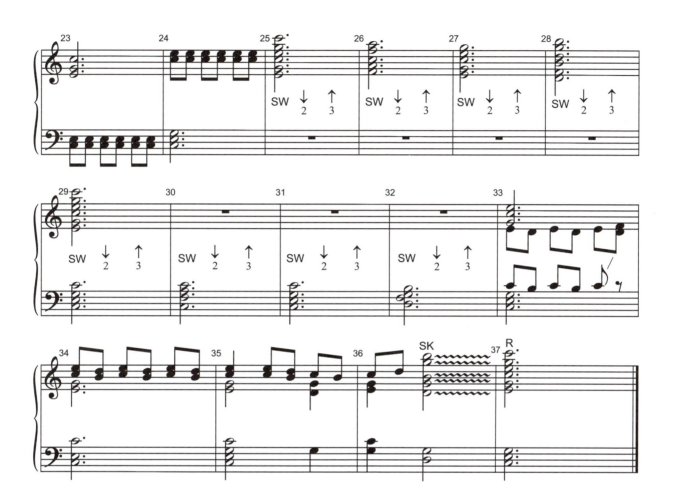

## Skill Twelve — The Swing

*"On the Water II" (3 oct)*

# On the Water II
### 3 octaves

Based on *WATER MUSIC*
G. F. Handel, 1685-1759
arr. Erin MacGorman

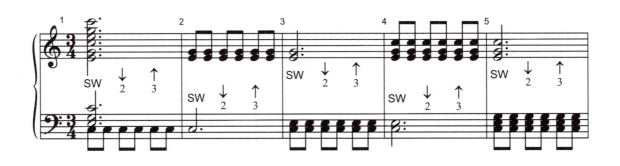

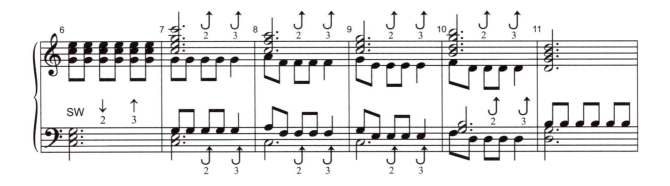

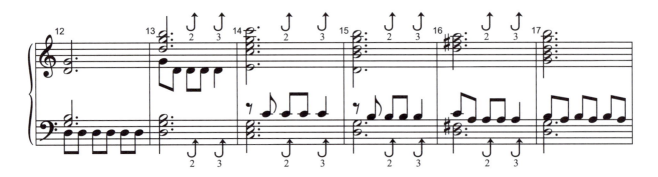

## Skill Twelve — The Swing

*"On the Water II" (3 oct)* continued

## Skill Twelve — The Swing

### Musical Examples — Two Octaves

*"On the Water I" (2 oct)*

# On the Water I
### 2 octaves

Based on *WATER MUSIC*
G. F. Handel, 1685-1759
arr. Erin MacGorman

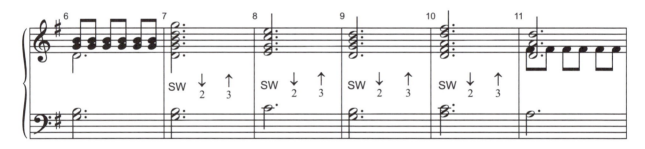

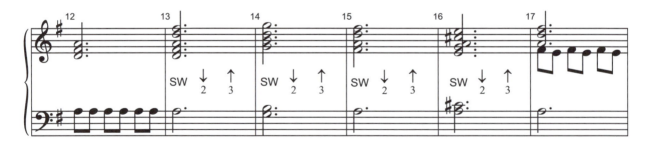

# Skill Twelve — The Swing

*"On the Water I" (2 oct)* continued

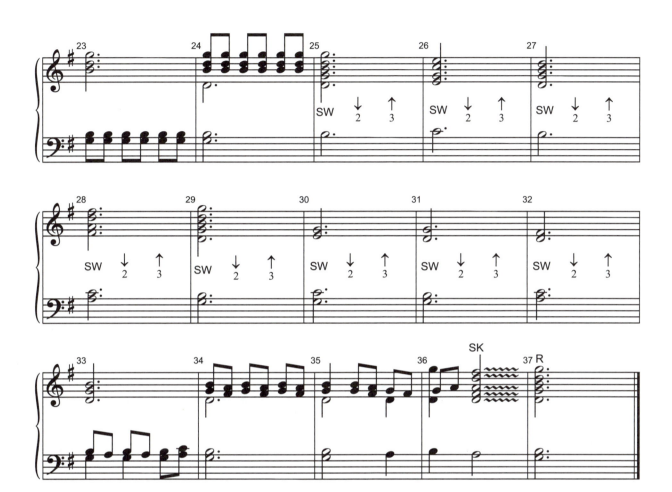

# Skill Twelve — The Swing

*"On the Water II" (2 oct)*

## Skill Twelve — The Swing

*"On the Water II" (2 oct)* continued

# Skill Thirteen
## Let Vibrate

**LV**   "Let Vibrate" passages are often used in handbell music to instruct the ringers not to damp. As harmonies change, one "LV" ends and another one begins. There are three ways to signal the end of an "LV" passage:

1. another "LV" **LV**
2. "R" **R**
3. damp sign ⊕

### Rote Exercise

Ringers take their two natural bells. (Two octave choirs may have the F ringers take F#.) Establish a slow steady beat. On beat one, ringer 1 rings her left bell and **keeps it moving** making a large circle with the arm. On beat two, ringer 2 rings his left bell and **keeps it moving**, and so on up the table. Have the ringers repeat the drill using their right bells. The result is a "build up" of sound from not damping the bells.

# Skill Thirteen — Let Vibrate

## Musical Example — Three Octaves

*"Syrian Folk Song" (3 oct)*

# Skill Thirteen — Let Vibrate

## Musical Example — Two Octaves

*"Syrian Folk Song (2 oct)*

# Skill Fourteen
## Martellato and Martellato Lift

**Rote Exercise #1**

*Martellato* ▼

Ringers take their two natural bells. (Two octave choirs should have the F ringers take F#.) Hold the bells parallel to the table about two inches above the table. Execute the martellato by pressing the bell into the foam so that the sound completely stops. (This action may be described as "bury the knuckles in the foam.") Ringer 1 martellatos the left bell twice in half notes then repeats with the right bell. All other ringers pantomime this action. Ringer 1 joins the others in pantomime after he completes the drill, as ringer 2 executes the martellato. Continue the exercise until all ringers have completed a turn.

Encourage ringers to make certain the sound of the bell is completely stopped in the foam. As the ringers pantomime, they become aware of the feel and appearance of the martellato.

**Rote Exercise #2**

*Martellato Lift* ▼↑

Execute the martellato lift by quickly pressing the bell into the foam so that the sound does not completely stop. Immediately bring the bell back to the "preparatory position" if it is to be followed by another martellato, or to the "ready to ring" position if the next note is to be rung. Repeat the exercise used in the martellato technique replacing "martellato" with "martellato lift." Finally, vary the exercise by using the rhythm of a half note followed by two quarter notes.

## Note for Handchime Choirs

Do not use these two techniques with handchimes; they will damage the chimes. When a martellato or martellato lift appears in the music, use the stopped technique presented in Skill 8 (page 38).

# Skill Fourteen — Martellato and Martellato Lift

## Musical Example — Three Octaves

*"Hyfrydol" (3 oct)*

## Skill Fourteen — Martellato and Martellato Lift

*"Hyfrydol" (3 oct)* continued

# Skill Fourteen — Martellato and Martellato Lift

*"Hyfrydol" (3 oct)* continued

## Skill Fourteen — Martellato and Martellato Lift

### Musical Example — Two Octaves

*"Hyfrydol" (2 oct)*

# Skill Fourteen — Martellato and Martellato Lift

*"Hyfrydol" (2 oct)* continued

# Skill Fourteen — Martellato and Martellato Lift

*"Hyfrydol" (2 oct)* continued

# Skill Fifteen
## Using Mallets

### Rote Exercise #1
*Malleting Bells on the Table* ✝

Ringers take their two natural bells. Have the ringers place the head of the mallet on the bell at the point where they will strike it (just under the rim). Establish a slow, steady beat by counting, "one, two, one, two …"

On "one," have the ringers raise the mallet head 2"-3" above the bell keeping the mallet handle parallel to the table. On "two," mallets should strike the bell and bounce back in place (2"-3" above the bell).

### Rote Exercise #2
*Malleting Suspended Bells* ✚

Each ringer holds the left natural bell as usual and suspends the right natural bell from the little finger (or last two fingers) of the left hand. Holding the mallet parallel to the table, 2"-3" from the left bell, ringers should lightly strike the bell at the rim. As before, the mallet should bounce back to its starting position. Repeat until all ringers can strike their left bells precisely together. Repeat the exercise using the right bells. Finally, repeat alternating between left and right bells.

## Note for Handchime Choirs

It is not common practice to mallet handchimes. To simulate malleting bells resting on the table, use the stopped techniques for handchimes presented in Skill 8 (page 38). To simulate the effect of malleting suspended bells, ring handchimes softly without damping.

# Skill Fifteen — Using Mallets

## Musical Examples — Three Octaves

*"Amazing Grace" (3 oct)*

# Skill Fifteen — Using Mallets

*"Amazing Grace"* (*3 oct*) continued

# Skill Fifteen — Using Mallets

*"Puer Nobis" (3 oct)*

# Skill Fifteen — Using Mallets

*"Puer Nobis"* (3 oct) continued

# Skill Fifteen — Using Mallets

*"All My Heart This Night Rejoices"* (3 oct)

# Skill Fifteen — Using Mallets

*"All My Heart This Night Rejoices"* (*3 oct*) continued

# Skill Fifteen — Using Mallets

## Musical Examples — Two Octaves

*"Amazing Grace" (2 oct)*

86

# Skill Fifteen — Using Mallets

*"Amazing Grace" (2 oct)* continued

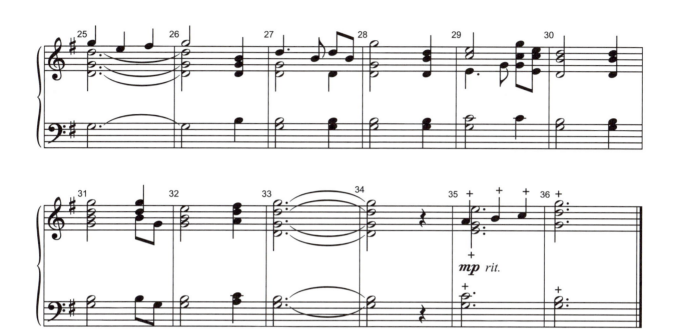

## Skill Fifteen — Using Mallets

*"Puer Nobis" (2 oct)*

# Skill Fifteen — Using Mallets

"*Puer Nobis*" *(2 oct)* continued

# Skill Fifteen — Using Mallets

*"All My Heart This Night Rejoices"* (2 oct)

# Skill Fifteen — Using Mallets

***"All My Heart This Night Rejoices"*** *(2 oct)* continued

# Choristers Guild Handbell Music

## Levels 1 and 2 with Related Techniques

### Levels 1 and 1+

| Title and Composer/Arranger | Octaves | Code | SK | TD | PI | ♪ | LV | ▼ | ▼↑ | ┼ | + | SW | RT |
|---|---|---|---|---|---|---|---|---|---|---|---|---|---|
| Bells of Christmas, The - arr. Moklebust | 2 | CGB146 | X | | | | X | | | | | | |
| Chords for Carols - arr. M. Tucker | 2, 3, 4 or 5 | CGB261 | X | | | | | | | | | | |
| Christmas Joy (Three Carol Settings) - arr. Ingram | 2-3 | CGB303 | X | X | | X | X | X | | | | | |
| Creator of the Stars of Night - arr. Moklebust | 2-3 | CGB268 | | | | | X | | | | X | | |
| Five Spirituals - arr. Ingram | 2-3 | CGB267 | X | X | X | X | X | | X | O | | X | |
| Harmonies for Hymns - arr. M. Tucker | 2, 3, 4 or 5 | CGB251 | X | | | | X | | | | | | |
| How Firm a Foundation - arr. Eithun | 2-3 | CGB305 | X | X | | | | | X | X | | | |
| I Have Decided to Follow Jesus - arr. Lamb | 3 | CGB279 | X | X | | X | | | | | | | |
| Jesus, Jesus, Rest Your Head - arr. Moklebust | 2-3 | CGB240 | | | | | X | | | | | | |
| Joyful Rhythm - McChesney | 2-3 | CGB219 | | | | | | | | | | | |
| Let Happy Hosannas Ring - Waldrop | 3 | CGB276 | X | X | X | | X | | | | | | |
| Meditations on the Cross - arr. Ingram | 2-3 | CGB277 | | | | X | X | X | | | | | |
| Of the Father's Love Begotten - arr. Turner | 2 | CGB197 | | | | | X | | | | | | |
| Processional and Bell Chime - M. Tucker | 3 | CGB319 | X | | | X | X | | | | | | |
| Ring Merrily - Kinyon | 2-3 | CGB106 | X | | | | | | | | | | |
| That Easter Day with Joy Was Bright (On Jordan's Banks the Baptist's Cry; What Star Is This, with Beams So Bright) - arr. Moklebust | 2-3 | CGB281 | | X | | | X | | | | | | |
| Three Hymns for Worship - arr. Ingram | 2-3 | CGB241 | | | | X | | | | | O | | |
| Three Hymns of Praise - arr. Ingram | 2-3 | CGB224 | X | | | X | X | | X | | | X | |
| What a Friend We Have in Jesus - arr. Geschke | 3 | CGB280 | | | | X | X | | | | | | |

### Levels 2 and 2+

| Title and Composer/Arranger | Octaves | Code | SK | TD | PI | ♪ | LV | ▼ | ▼↑ | ┼ | + | SW | RT |
|---|---|---|---|---|---|---|---|---|---|---|---|---|---|
| Advent Carol - arr. Hopson | 3 or 5 | CGB154 | X | | X | | X | | | | X | | |
| All Creatures Great and Small - Waldrop | 2-3 | CGB304 | X | | | X | X | | X | X | | | |
| All Glory, Laud and Honor - M. Tucker | 3, 4 or 5 | CGB245 | X | | | | X | | | | | | |
| All Through the Night - arr. Kinyon | 2 | CGB158 | | | | | X | | | | | | |
| Amazing Grace - arr. Moklebust (Handbell Score) | 3, 4 or 5 with opt. Organ | CGB201 | X | | | | X | | | | | | |
| As Lately We Watched - arr. Ingram | 3, 4 or 5 | CGB308 | | | | X | | | | | | | |
| Awesome Adoration - Geschke | 3 | CGB259 | X | | | | X | X | X | | | X | X |
| Be Thou My Vision - arr. Moklebust | 3, 4 or 5 oct. bell choir and 2-3 oct. chime choir | CGB286 | | | X | | X | | | | X | | |
| Carillon Chimes - Boynton | 2 | CGB108 | | X | | | X | | | | | | |
| Carol of the Bells - arr. Moklebust | 2 | CGB164 | | | | | | | | | | | |

*Visit our website, www.choristersguild.org, for an up-to-date version of this list.*

# Choristers Guild Handbell Music — Levels 1 and 2 with Related Techniques

| Publication Information | | | X = Technique Used;  O = Optional Technique | | | | | | | | | |
|---|---|---|---|---|---|---|---|---|---|---|---|---|
| Title and Composer/Arranger | Octaves | Code | SK | TD | PI | ↧ | LV | ▼ | ▼↑ | ✝ | + | SW | RT |
| Carry Me Home - arr. Loiacono | 3 | CGB180 | | | X | | | | | | | | |
| Children of the Heavenly Father - arr. Moklebust | 3 | CGB139 | | | | | X | | | | | | |
| Christians, We Have Met to Worship - arr. S. Tucker | 3 | CGB209 | | X | | | X | X | | | | | |
| Christmas Bell Fanfare - Wagner | 2 | CGB36 | X | | | | X | | | | | X | |
| Christmas Joy Fanfare - Wagner | 2-3 | CGB100 | X | | | | X | X | | | | | |
| Come Away/Swing Low - arr. Smith | 3, 4 or 5 | CGB285 | X | | | | X | X | | | | | |
| Come, Christians, Join to Sing - McKechnie | 3 | CGB90 | X | | | | X | | | | | | |
| Come Into God's Presence with Ringing - Bedford | 3 or 5 | CGB183 | X | X | X | | X | | | | | | |
| Come, Thou Long-Expected Jesus - arr. Moklebust | 2-3 | CGB266 | | O | O | | | X | | | O | | |
| Come, Thou Long-Expected Jesus - arr. Thompson | 3-4 | CGB86 | X | | | | X | | | | | | |
| Earth Shall Ring (PERSONENT HODIE) - M. Tucker | 3, 4 or 5 | CGB214 | X | | | | X | | | X | | | |
| Easter Alleluia - arr. Nelson | 3, 4 or 5 | CGB216 | X | | | | X | | | X | | | |
| Fanfare and Alleluia - Wagner | 2 | CGB41 | X | | | | X | | | | | X | |
| Fanfare for Bells - McCleary | 4-5 | CGB14 | | | | | X | | | | | | |
| Festive Variations - Helman (4-5 Octave Edition) | 4-5 | CGB256 | | | | X | | X | | X | | | X |
| Festive Variations - Helman (2-3 Octave Edition) | 2-3 | CGB247 | | | | X | | X | | X | | | X |
| First Noel, The - arr. McChesney | 2-3 | CGB199 | | | | X | X | | | | | | |
| Gloria - Mozart/arr. Thompson (Ringers' Score) | 3 and organ | CGB121 | X | | | | | | | | | | |
| God's Grace, All Sufficient - arr. M. Tucker | 3, 4 or 5 | CGB236 | X | | | | X | | | | | | |
| Good King Wenceslas - arr. Eithun | 3, 4 or 5 | CGB271 | X | X | | | X | X | X | X | X | | |
| Greensleeves - arr. Moklebust | 3, 4 or 5 oct. bell choir and 2-3 oct. chime choir | CGB322 | | | | X | X | | | | | | |
| Holly and the Ivy, The - arr. McChesney | 3 | CGB137 | | | | | X | | | | | | |
| Holy God, We Praise Your Name - arr. Page | 3, 4 or 5 | CGB287 | X | | | X | X | | | X | | | |
| Holy Manna - arr. McChesney | 2 | CGB123 | X | | | | X | | | | | | |
| How Can I Keep From Singing? - arr. Burkhardt/trans. Finnigan | 4-5 | CGB265 | | | | | X | | X | | | X | |
| Hymn to Joy - arr. Story | 3 | CGB163 | X | | | | | | | | | | |
| I Will Arise and Go to Jesus - arr. Edwards | 3 or 5 | CGB264 | X | | | | | X | | X | | | |
| Immortal, Invisible, God Only Wise - arr. Kinyon | 3 | CGB172 | | | | | X | | | | | | |
| In the Bleak Midwinter - arr. Moklebust | 3, 4 or 5 oct. bell choir and 2-3 oct. chime choir | CGB260 | | | | | X | | | | | X | |
| Infant Holy, Infant Lowly - arr. Moklebust | 2-3 | CGB222 | | | | | X | | | | | | |

# Choristers Guild Handbell Music — Levels 1 and 2 with Related Techniques

| Publication Information | | | X = Technique Used; O = Optional Technique | | | | | | | | | |
|---|---|---|---|---|---|---|---|---|---|---|---|---|
| Title and Composer/Arranger | Octaves | Code | SK | TD | PI | ↥ | LV | ▼ | ▼↑ | ✢ | + | SW | RT |
| Irish Melody, An - arr. M. Tucker | 3, 4 or 5 | CGB289 | | | | | X | | | | X | | |
| Joyous Alleluia, A - Geschke | 3 | CGB226 | X | | | | | X | X | | | X | |
| Jubilant Fanfare - McChesney | 2-3 | CGB141 | X | | | | | X | X | | | | |
| Lamb of God (Agnus Dei) - Moklebust | 3, 4 or 5 oct. bell choir and 2-3 oct. chime choir | CGB254 | | | | | | X | | | | | |
| Land of Rest - arr. McChesney | 3, 4 or 5 | CGB215 | | | | | | X | | | | | |
| Let All Mortal Flesh Keep Silence - arr. Mizell | 3-4 with hammered dulcimer or other inst. | CGB301 | | | | X | X | | | X | X | | |
| Let Us Break Bread Together - arr. Edwards | 3 | CGB227 | | | | | | | | | | | |
| Lord's My Shepherd, The - Geschke | 3 | CGB243 | | | | | | X | | | | X | |
| Mary Had a Baby - arr. Page | 3, 4 or 5 | CGB238 | | | | X | X | | | | | | |
| Meditation - Edwards | 2-3 | CGB220 | | X | | | | | | | | X | X |
| Meditation on Hyfrydol - arr. S. Tucker | 3 | CGB182 | | | | | | X | | | | | |
| Morning Canticle - S. Tucker | 2-3 | CGB233 | X | | X | | | X | | | | | X |
| Quiet Alleluia, A - Livingston | 3 | CGB115 | | X | | | | X | | | | | |
| Quiet Reflections - Edwards | 2-3 | CGB231 | | X | O | | | | | O | | X | |
| Rejoice Greatly - Geschke (2-3 Octave Edition) | 2-3 | CGB284 | X | | | | | X | X | | | | |
| Rejoice Greatly - Geschke (4-5 Octave Edition) | 4-5 | CGB302 | X | | X | | | X | X | | | | |
| Rise Up, Shepherd, and Follow (Advent and Christmas Pieces Based on American Folk Melodies) - arr. Moklebust | 2-3 | CGB184 | X | O | O | | X | X | | O | X | | X |
| Savior of the Nations, Come - arr. Moklebust (3, 4 or 5 Oct. Edition) | 3, 4 or 5 | CGB300 | | | | | | X | | | | X | |
| Savior of the Nations, Come - arr. Moklebust (2-3 Oct. Edition) | 2-3 | CGB173 | | | | | | X | | | | X | |
| Shall We Gather at the River - arr. M. Tucker | 3, 4 or 5 | CGB298 | | | | | | X | | | | | |
| Sheltering Wings - Edwards | 3 | CGB187 | | | | | | X | | | | | |
| Shepherd's Psalm, The - Kerr | 3, 4 or 5 | CGB116 | | | | | | X | | | | X | |
| Shining Bright - arr. Lamb | 2-3 | CGB282 | X | X | | | | X | | | | | |
| Silent Night - arr. Kliever | 2-3 | CGB150 | | | | | | | | | | | |
| Simple Suite, A - McChesney | 2-3 | CGB235 | | | O | X | X | X | | O | | | |
| Song of Reflection - Edwards | 3 | CGB283 | | | | | | | | | X | | |
| Song of the Angels - arr. Page | 2-3 | CGB176 | X | | O | | X | | | O | | | |
| Sounds of Joy - Geschke | 2-3 | CGB217 | X | X | | X | X | X | | | | X | |
| Still, Still, Still - arr. Moklebust | 2-3 | CGB210 | | | | | | X | | | | | |
| This Day of Gladness - Geschke | 2-3 | CGB208 | X | | | | | X | X | | | | |
| Thee We Adore (Four Lent/Communion and Easter Pieces) - arr. Moklebust | 2 | CGB166 | | X | X | X | X | | | | | | X |
| Timbrel and Dance - McChesney | 3, 4 or 5 | CGB290 | X | X | | | X | | | X | | | |
| Triumphant Exultation - Edwards | 2 | CGB142 | X | X | | | X | | | | | | X |
| 'Twas in the Moon of Wintertime - arr. Moklebust | 2-3 | CGB155 | | O | O | X | X | | | O | | | |

# Choristers Guild Handbell Music — Levels 1 and 2 with Related Techniques

| Publication Information | | | X = Technique Used;  O = Optional Technique | | | | | | | | | |
|---|---|---|---|---|---|---|---|---|---|---|---|---|
| Title and Composer/Arranger | Octaves | Code | SK | TD | PI | ↥ | LV | ▼ | ▼↑ | ⁚ | + | SW | RT |
| Two Carols for Handbells and Organ - Ferguson | 3, 4 or 5 | CGB273 | | | | | X | | | | | | |
| Variations on a French Carol - arr. Edwards | 2 | CGB246 | X | X | | | X | | | | | | X |
| We Gather Together - arr. Angerman | 3, 4 or 5 | CGB270 | | | | | X | | | | | | |
| Welsh Folk Tune, A - arr. M. Tucker | 3 | CGB159 | | | | | X | | | | | | |
| Were You There? - arr. Edwards | 3 | CGB274 | | | | | | | | | | X | |
| What Is This Lovely Fragrance? - arr. Moklebust | 2-3 | CGB178 | | | | | X | | | | | | |
| What Star Is This That Beams So Bright - arr. Kinyon | 2 | CGB111 | | | | | | | | | | | |

## Other Instructional Resources From Choristers Guild

### Let's Ring Chimes and Bells
A Workbook for Beginning Chime and Handbell Ringers
by Kirtsy Mitchell
(CGBK48)

### Basic Rhythms For Bell Choirs
36 Exercises in Rhythmic Unison For Beginning Bell Choirs
by Page C. Long
(CGB40)

### Music For a Beginning Handbell Choir
With Study Plans
(Fourth Grade Through Adult)
by D. Linda McKechnie
(CGB57)

# Index of Songs

| | 3 octaves | 2 octaves |
|---|---|---|
| All My Heart This Night Rejoices | 84 | 90 |
| Amazing Grace | 80 | 86 |
| Count the Rests! | 13 | 15 |
| Dance of the Hours | 40 | 42 |
| Evening Prayer | 57 | 58 |
| Fairest Lord Jesus | 29 | 30 |
| God Is So Good | 14 | 16 |
| God of the Ages | 32 | 33 |
| Happy or Sad? | 24 | 26 |
| Hyfrydol | 72 | 75 |
| Jesus Shall Reign – Preparatory Exercise | 18 | 21 |
| Jesus Shall Reign I | 19 | 22 |
| Jesus Shall Reign II | 20 | 23 |
| Little David | 45 | 47 |
| Lord, Have Mercy | 49 | 52 |
| Morning Bells I | 7 | 10 |
| Morning Bells II | 8 | 11 |
| Morning Bells III | 9 | n/a |
| Old Ship of Zion | 39 | 41 |
| On the Water I | 60 | 64 |
| On the Water II | 62 | 66 |
| Processional | 35 | 36 |
| Puer Nobis | 82 | 88 |
| Scarborough Fair | 44 | 46 |
| Syrian Folk Song | 69 | 70 |
| We, Thy People, Praise Thee | 50 | 54 |